First published in Great Britain by HarperCollinsEntertainment 2005
HarperCollinsEntertainment is a division of HarperCollinsPublishers Ltd,
77 – 85 Fulham Palace Road, Hammersmith, London, W6 8JB

The HarperCollins children's website address is
www.harpercollinschildrensbooks.co.uk

The Mary-Kate and Ashley website address is
www.mary-kateandashley.com

1 3 5 7 9 10 8 6 4 2

ISBN 0-00-720982-7

Printed and bound in China

mary–kateandashley

style secrets

...what to wear and how to wear it

www.mary-kateandashley.com

DUALSTAR
PUBLICATIONS

HarperCollins*Entertainment*
An imprint of HarperCollinsPublishers

mary–kateandashley

style secrets

...what to wear and how to wear it

www.mary-kateandashley.com

DUALSTAR
PUBLICATIONS

HarperCollins*Entertainment*
An imprint of HarperCollinsPublishers

Hi.

Welcome to our Style Secrets!

We know you love fashion as much as we do, so we've put together this book for you with help from the executive designer from our fashion line, Judy Swartz. It includes fashion hints and tips we've learned over the years, with seven sections that show you how to make the most of your wardrobe.

Have fun!

Mary-Kate Ashley

contents

1 what every girl needs

"Fashion is always changing and that's why I find it so interesting. A few basic pieces go a long way in any wardrobe.... I'm partial to my favourite white shirt, vintage Levis and a simple black dress." Ashley

It's easy to look good every day but, like anything else, you have to put some preparation into it. By building a good basic wardrobe, you will always have the basis of a great outfit. Everyday pieces like black trousers, white shirts and jeans can be dressed up or down with one or two additions, like a hip jacket or glitzy scarf. Once you've got the basics down, the rest is easy!

Mixing and matching is more than half the fun of fashion. Why not take an afternoon to go through all your clothes and see what's hiding in the back of your wardrobe – you might discover some fashion finds you'd forgotten you had. When you add these pieces to your basics, you've got your very own one-of-a-kind collection!

classic five pocket jeans

✳ Classic indigo, five pocket jeans are a no brainer – you probably already own at least one pair. These are the basis for a million hot outfits.

The best basic jean should:

✳ Sit just below the waist

✳ Have a button-up fly

✳ Fit closely through the thigh and knee without being uncomfortable

✳ Be a bootleg cut

✳ Sit halfway down your foot when you're wearing boots

black trousers

※ Black trousers come in just behind jeans in the useful stakes. They are slightly dressier than jeans and can be worn for a dozen different occasions.

※ Again, a slight flare in the leg is the most flattering cut. Avoid a jean-style cut and choose either wide leg or hipsters with a bit of a kick. Don't buy them too long though, the last thing you want is a frayed hem on smart black trousers.

※ A heavier weight material is best as anything too thin will rub up and won't last very long. Not good for an item in your capsule collection!

white shirt

✳ A white shirt is a great wardrobe staple. On its own, a white shirt makes every outfit look clean and smart.

✳ A really great white shirt will have a high thread count, be fitted at the waist and won't have any pockets.

✳ For a bit of old-school cool, wear your shirt with a loosely knotted tie, jeans, baseball boots and a blazer or leather jacket.

✳ White shirts are great and go with everything. But if you have trouble keeping your spaghetti sauce on your plate and off your clothes, maybe a black shirt would be a better option. It's just as smart and won't stain as easily as a white cotton shirt!

 +  = *cool*

pencil skirt

☀ A pencil skirt is so flexible! Opt for a dark colour in a heavy material to get the most wear out of it. A bit of stretch will also help it keep its shape better (and avoid some ironing!).

☀ A black, khaki or denim pencil skirt cut to the knee will look great with any footwear –party shoes, trainers, knee boots or even flip-flops.

☀ For a casual look, add one of your T-shirts and denim jacket. For an instant dose of smart, wear with your white shirt and a V-neck sweater.

☀ A sundress with a pencil skirt-style cut is also a good buy. You can wear it alone in summer, pull on a little sweater in winter or even wear a T-shirt or shirt over the top to create a completely different look.

+ = *casual*

sweaters

✳ V-neck sweaters look fab on their own and super smart with a shirt underneath.

✳ Always buy round neck sweaters in colours that really suit you as they are much closer to your face than V-necks.

✳ You can buy sweaters in dozens of different knits, shades and textures from every store on the high street. Wool and cotton are really wearable for every day and cashmere is completely luxurious!

| what every girl needs

basic t-shirts and vests

✳ T-shirts are one of the most inexpensive and versatile items in your capsule wardrobe. EVERYONE should own a classic white and classic black, round neck, short sleeve T-shirt. It goes with everything!

✳ Vests are another essential staple. Go for a good quality black cotton tank top and a strappy white vest. They can be worn on their own or layered with other shirts, T-shirts and sweaters.

✳ Long-sleeved T-shirts are perfect for spring. Try layering plain colours and a contrasting printed short sleeved T-shirt over the top.

coat

✳ A classic coat is a real investment buy, so choose carefully. You need to be able to get a lot of wear out of it, so pick a neutral colour like black or camel. If you're a pattern fan, choose a classic herringbone, houndstooth check or tweed.

✳ A classic trench coat or a button-up wool coat will look great dressed up or down.

✳ If you're mad about a certain colour, then go for it but don't spend a lot of money on a bright green coat if you're likely to be nuts about hot pink next season!

low-heeled boot

✳ Low-heeled boots are a great alternative to trainers. Brown or black leather are the most versatile with a zip fastening up the inside of the leg.

✳ Go for either a mid-calf or a knee height to get the most wear out of your boots. That way, you can wear them with trousers and skirts.

✳ When the heel starts to wear down, go to your nearest shoe maker and get the boots re-heeled. It doesn't cost much money, can be done in under an hour and it will make your boots last much longer.

party shoe

✳ Your basic party shoes need to be ready to go whenever you need them, so they have to go with everything in your wardrobe – skirts, trousers and dresses.

✳ However much you love those bright pink shoes, they probably aren't right for your capsule wardrobe. A pair of black shoes with a mid-height heel are perfect – never go too high, you don't know if you'll be dancing all night or sitting down to eat.

✳ The heel should be slender and go for something strappy but supportive at the front. You don't want to be falling out of your shoes all night!

2 hanging out

"Nothing beats comfy drawstring pants! Ashley and I love to dress casual and comfy." Mary-Kate

Hands up, who hasn't woken up on a Saturday morning and just thrown on sweat pants and a hoodie? We thought so, because we definitely have! But there is a way to look cool and casual at the same time.

By having the right pieces in your wardrobe, there's no reason you can't be a style goddess when you're at the mall, on the beach or even just hanging out with your friends.

Instead of creased sweat pants, an old T-shirt and dirty trainers, think cropped trousers and a polo shirt with fun flip-flops. Going shopping? It's got to be easy to get in and out of and not crease too easily. How about a gypsy skirt, a vintage tee and sandals? Casual is cool!

sweat pants

❋ Sweat pants are brilliant for slouching around the house and come in all sorts of fun colours! Team them with flip-flops or clean trainers and a fun T-shirt.

❋ Don't buy anything too long– if you are planning to exercise, you don't want to trip over your pants, do you?

❋ Look for pants with a deep waistband that are not too low on the hips, these are the most flattering and they won't fall down when you run!

+ = *comfort*

cute and cropped tees

❋ There are a hundreds of different types of T-shirts out there. We love vintage-style printed T-shirts which you can buy anywhere. Look in second-hand stores for genuine vintage. We think old band T-shirts are best.

❋ You can try lots of different shapes with T-shirts – cropped, V-neck, slash-neck and boat-necks as well as the classic round crew neck. And do you want short sleeves, long sleeves, cap sleeves or no sleeves? The choice is endless!

❋ Make sure you take care of your T-shirts. Wash, hang dry, iron and fold them properly or they can easily lose their shape.

trainers

✳ The best way to stop your trainers looking scruffy is to keep them clean. Once a week or so, clean them with a special trainer whitener and use trainer fresheners to stop them getting stinky!

✳ Vintage-style fashion trainers look great with jeans and T-shirts but they're not good for sport. If you're going to be running around, you need to go to the sports store and get the right shoes for your sport.

✳ Baseball boots are really hot right now and look great with cropped jeans, a vest and heaps of bracelets – very rock! You can get them in loads of colours and patterns and they make a change from boring white trainers.

jackets

※ A casual jacket should be something you can just throw on without thinking too much about it. A zip-up, collarless jacket in a neutral colour looks great with all of your casual clothes.

※ Beat-up leather and denim jackets also look good for casual wear. Try those vintage and second hand shops again rather than paying more for a new jacket made to look old.

※ If you're just hanging out with your friends or on the way to the gym, a tracksuit top to match your sweatpants can look cute. But a word of warning: don't wear the matching velour suit, especially with heels – that look is so over!

printed shirts

✳ Just like your white shirt, a printed shirt is really versatile and a can be a lot of fun. A checked, western-cut shirt looks great with jeans and once it starts looking a little tired, you can cut the sleeves off for a new look.

✳ A short-sleeved shirt with puffed cap sleeves is a really pretty, easy to wear look. Pair it with your pencil skirt, flip-flops and a tote bag for instant shopping style.

✳ For a fun look, wear a printed shirt over your swimsuit and shorts. The perfect cover up in the sun.

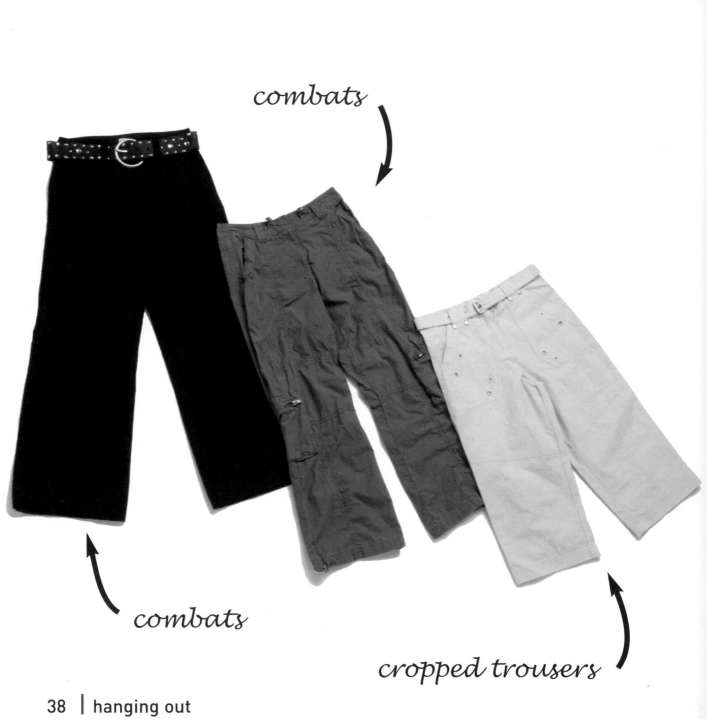

combats

combats

cropped trousers

trousers

✳ Combat trousers are great for casual style. Go for khaki or black – not camouflage print – and wear with a little T-shirt and a beat up jacket.

✳ Light cotton trousers are perfect for lazing around in summer. Wear a wide leg, drawstring waist and a light colour, even white if you can keep them clean!

✳ If you're not really a skirt or shorts girl, then cropped trousers are for you. Casual with flip-flops and a tee, punk with a black vest and baseball boots, they go with everything!

ponchos and wraps

✳ We love wraps! They go with absolutely everything, come in loads of colours and fabrics and can be rolled up in your day bag for when they're needed.

✳ The most versatile kind of wrap is a pashmina. Try black or cream wool with your jeans and a white T-shirt. Be sure to store it in a plastic bag to stop the moths from getting to the wool.

✳ Ponchos are a fun alternative to a jacket and a real blast from the past. If you can't find what you're looking for in the stores, head for the second hand shops or ask your family. They might have some vintage gems tucked away somewhere!

bikinis, swimsuits and tankinis

✳ A bikini is fun if you're just going to be sunbathing or splashing around in the pool, but if you're going to be doing any real swimming or running around, go for a sleek swimsuit.

✳ Tankini's are the perfect compromise between a bikini and swimsuit. Roll the vest up to get a tanned tum and roll it down for more coverage.

✳ The most important thing to remember when buying a swimsuit is to pick something you're super comfortable in whether it's classic black or a fun tropical print! Be careful if you're wearing a white swimsuit. If it's not lined, it could go transparent when wet!

flip-flops and sandals

✳ Flip-flops are the ideal shoe for summer days. Pick a thong style–preferably leather – in a fun colour that will match all your outfits – black, brown, pale pink and baby blue are all good bets.

✳ If you're going on holiday, think about foam flip-flops. They can be decorated to suit any outfit and they cost next to nothing so you can dump them once you're through, which means less packing!

✳ There are so many styles of sandals it's hard to know where to start, but wooden sandals with a leather strap across the front are classics that never seem to go out of fashion.

3 go for glam

"We love dressing up for special occasions and Hollywood events! To complete our look, we like to find a special piece of vintage jewellery or a stylish handbag." Mary-Kate and Ashley

This is one of our favourite styles. We love to get dressed up! But getting glammed up doesn't necessarily mean buying a brand new sparkly dress, skyscraper heels and wearing all your jewellery at once.

OK, sometimes it means buying a new dress (any excuse to shop!) but really, glamorous clothes are all about the fabrics, the embellishments, the cut and the shape. Even a pair of jeans can be glamorous when teamed with sparkly shoes and a gorgeous top – there's no point spending a fortune on a gorgeous dress if you are never normally out of trousers.

The most important thing to remember when you're picking an outfit for a dressy occasion is to choose something that you will be comfortable in all night long and something that you love!

dresses

A little black dress goes a long way. Go for something plain that ends just below the knee and then how you accessorise it is entirely up to you. This outfit will be perfect for black tie events, holiday parties, birthday parties and any unexpected events!

If you're going for colour, be bold. Deep red is very dramatic and pastels look romantic in the summer.

Dresses can look really hip with jeans. Flapper-style dresses, vintage tunics and asymmetric hems look fab over jeans with sandals or party heels.

blazers and suits

❋ A suit might sound like something your dad would wear for work but they can look stunning for a really classy night out. Either a black tuxedo or a white linen suit teamed with a contrasting, silky top look fantastic.

❋ Separate the suit for even more great outfits! Black satin tuxedo pants can be teamed up with almost anything for an instant glam look.

❋ The suit jacket or a beautiful blazer plays down a glitzy top and jeans for a stylin' party look.

detail, detail!

✳ The main difference between glam and casual clothes is the detail. Look for lace edging, subtle frills and embroidery.

✳ Fabrics will be more luxurious – silk, satin, velvet, fine knits, cashmere. These all need special care to look their best!

✳ You can add detail to a more basic top to really make it your own. Try pinning a fresh corsage to your suit jacket or adding some lace trim to the hem of a tired looking sweater.

sparkle and sequins

✳ Anything glitzy really does scream nightime glam – just remember, less is more and never over do it.

✳ An all-over glitter or sequinned top looks fab with a completely plain skirt or trousers, plain black heels and your blazer.

✳ A touch of sparkle on your skirt will really catch the light while you're dancing without being completely overpowering.

when bad things happen to good clothes

- Clothes should never have to suffer like this...
- Think about where you're going. Is dry clean only silk a good idea for a family barbecue?
- If there's going to be a punch bowl and a ladle where you're going, think twice about wearing white.
- If the worst should happen to your party clothes, check the label inside for what to do. Never put silk in the washing machine and always try and dab out stains with cold water. Hot water will just set the stain more quickly.

4

it's in the jeans

"There are so many great pairs of jeans out there, but finding the perfect fit isn't easy. Mary-Kate and I usually have our favourite jeans tailored to ensure the most flattering look and fit." Ashley

From skinny drainpipe jeans to long denim coats and everything in between, everyone has some denim in their wardrobe and it's really what you do with it that counts.

Everyone loves jeans from students to Hollywood celebs. You are just as likely to see blue denim on the red carpet as the street because it is one of the most versatile materials around.

Do you dress up your jeans with a sparkly top or throw your faded denim jacket over a feminine tea dress? And what kind of jeans to choose? Stone washed, indigo, tinted, vintage, blue, black, cropped, flared, bootcut, even eighties acid wash! The list is endless. You can be really experimental with denim without going too far wrong.

different styles of jeans

❖ Once you've got your classic five pocket jeans, start looking further afield. Drainpipe jeans are very cool and look great in a dark denim, tucked into the tops of your boots.

❖ For a real pop princess look, a faded, distressed hipster jean is perfect. These look just as hot with vintage T-shirts and baseball boots as with a glam top and sparkling party shoes.

❖ Denim overalls come in and out of fashion, but if you're just hanging out they're really fun. Try teaming them with a cute, pink T-shirt and flip-flops to soften.

customise your denim

❖ It's easy to get an individual look for your jeans. If you're after a bit of grunge glamour, try letting down the hem and adding a few rips to the legs. No more than two rips each leg; you don't want your jeans to fall apart!

❖ If you're good with a needle, you can always embroider patterns onto your jeans. If not, go for iron-on patches and get someone to help you sew around the edges.

❖ For subtle sparkle, use washable glitter glue and highlight the pockets, fly and belt loops of your skirt. Voila! Revitalised party skirt!

denim jackets

❖ A basic denim jacket can be worn with hundreds of outfits but looks best contrasted against something really feminine and floaty, like a floral skirt or cute summer dress.

❖ For a more formal look, a denim blazer with lots of stretch in it looks fab with black trousers or cords. This look really works best with plain T-shirts and shirts under the jacket.

❖ One thing to avoid is wearing jeans and a denim jacket at the same time. Double denim is so not a good look.

customise your jacket

❖ Denim jackets look and feel best with age, so look for one that is already slightly distressed. If you have to buy new, give it a good bash around!

❖ For a cool look, add loads of fun badges to the lapels of the jacket. Try and find old badges. You can pick up loads in charity shops for next to nothing.

❖ Trim a denim blazer with ribbon for a ladylike look. Glue or sew it around the waist and the cuffs. Try a contrasting colour like baby pink if you want to stand out and baby blue if you want it to tone with your jacket.

what to wear with denim
- glam

❖ Jeans love heels and that's a fact. Go for a sparkly shoe that will peep out of the denim and make a statement all of its own – silver, green, gold – the choice is endless!

❖ A glitzy top really shines against simple denim. How many celebs have you seen on the red carpet in simple hipsters and a sparkling halter-top in the last few years? Heaps! Because it's simple and it works.

❖ With an easy, light denim base, you can go crazy with glam accessories. Black top and jeans, plus sparkly clutch, silver shoes, dozens of bangles and some dangly earrings and you're all glammed up and ready to go!

cords

❖ Cords are just as easy to wear as jeans but tend to be more acceptable when you can't really get away with denim. Earthy tones look fab and the material is really comfortable and hardwearing.

❖ Look for the same sorts of cuts as you would with jeans and wear with your boots. No fear of double denim here so throw your denim jacket on top.

❖ There are a lot more colour choices with cords. Browns look great for every day but you can really try anything. Deep reds, pinks, greens or tan. One rule, stay away from blues, they can look a little bit like wannabe jeans.

your c...

❖ Jeans can las[...]
if they do fail you[...]
them. You can al[...]
down to make cr[...]
shorts or a skirt [...]
with a needle.

❖ With the left [...]
you can make all [...]
accessories. Usin[...]
stitching you can [...]
covers, handbags, [...]
pencil cases. Trus[...]

5 a girl's guide to feeling good

"What you wear can definitely brighten your mood. I have a weakness for shoes and watches. When I'm wearing a new pair of heels and find the perfect vintage watch, I feel great!" Mary-Kate

We all know there are some girls out there who just have 'it'. They look great every day, their clothes are never creased, they always look like their clothes are made to measure and they all claim it took them practically no time to get ready.

Want to know a secret? It probably didn't. More than half of looking fabulous every day is down to preparation, taking care of your clothes, picking the right shapes for you and knowing what you're going to wear in advance.

Have a look through this section, then have a look at your wardrobe. Need an hour or so to tidy it up? Uh-huh, us too...

what shape suits me? – *bottoms*

✺ If your legs are a little on the short side you should really avoid cropped trousers as they will make your legs look shorter. On the plus side, you can get away with really tiny mini skirts as they won't look so tiny on your petite frame.

✺ If you're broader on top with slim legs, go for bootcut trousers and jeans and A-line skirts as the flare will balance you out.

✺ If your top half is tiny, you'll want to try and streamline your bottom half with slim-fitting trousers and skirts in darker colours.

no-no!

what shape suits me? –
tops

❀ If your top half is bigger than your bottom half, wear fitted tops with V-necks and ¾ length sleeves which will make you look more balanced.

❀ If you're tiny on top, you can wear big chunky polo necks and heavier fabrics. Gilets and ponchos look great on you!

❀ Fitted tops almost always look nicer than big baggy tops and T-shirts. Sweaters and fitted shirts suit everyone. The most important thing to do is to try before you buy and make sure your clothes fit!

organise your wardrobe

❀ Clear space on your bed and carefully pull out all of your clothes. Separate them into three piles – keep, throw away and charity. Anything you really love and wear all the time can be kept for now. If something is damaged beyond repair it goes in the throw away pile. The charity pile is for clothes you haven't worn in the last year but are in good repair. Be brutal about this one!

❀ If anything in your keep pile needs ironing, make a new pile and make sure they are all ironed properly before you put them away. Either hang everything in your wardrobe or fold neatly and put it in your drawers. No more piles by the bed!

❀ Organise your storage by type of clothes. Sweaters in one drawer, T-shirts in another, trousers and skirts all hung-up, etc.

taking care of your clothes

❀ Taking care of your clothes will make them last longer and look better. Always check the washing instructions before tossing stuff in the washing machine! You won't be happy when your expensive mohair sweater comes out half its original size.

❀ If you find a hole in your clothes or a hem comes loose, repair it straight away, don't just leave it to get worse. If it's a rip in your jeans, you can either cut them up into shorts or just go for the cool ripped jeans look!

❀ Iron your clothes on the recommended setting and put them straight away, leaving you with a wardrobe full of ready-to-wear clothes. Then you'll have no more last minute panics about what to wear!

6 accessories, accessories, accessories!

"When we were in high school we used accessories like jewellery, handbags and shoes to liven up our school uniforms. Now accessorising is just a way of life. When we travel, we love going to vintage stores and finding special pieces from around the world to add to our accessories collection."
Mary-Kate and Ashley

If there is one thing that can truly make or break an outfit, it is the accessories. Whether you're trying to liven up a basic outfit or really turn up the glamour, accessories are where it's at.

There are no hard and fast rules with accessorising and it is one area where you can really go for it – none of this less is more advice! If you want to turn an outfit from ladylike prim to ghetto fabulous, accessories are the key.

Imagine yourself in a pair of jeans and a white tank top. Add a leather cuff to each wrist and a thick studded belt on your hips. Now imagine the same outfit but with lots of boho beads around your neck and a chunky wooden bangle. See how easy it is to change your look with accessories?!

day bags

❀ Your day bag needs to be able to carry every little thing you might need in one day—mobile phone, diary, brush, make-up, keys, everything! So make sure it's big enough.

❀ There's no point having a gorgeous bag that you can't carry. Before you buy, make sure you can hook your dream day bag over your shoulder.

❀ You are likely to use this bag more than any other, so either make sure it will go with all your outfits or choose something that makes a real statement all on its own.

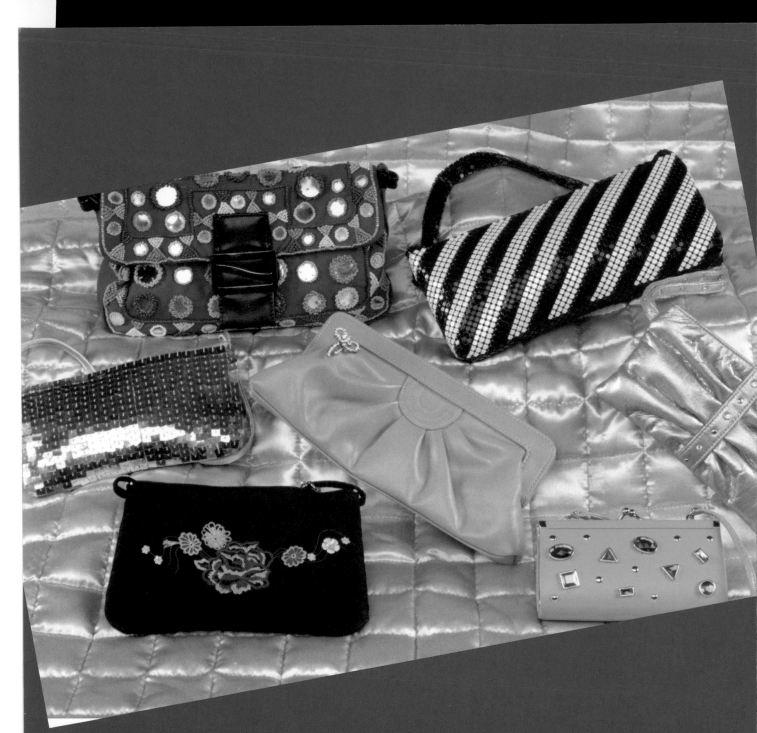

evening bags

❋ The first bag to look for is something moderately sized that will go with your basic black party shoes. A black leather clutch bag with a detachable handle will cover a lot of eventualities.

❋ Limit what you're going to put in the bag. Gorgeous tiny evening bags look silly if they're overstuffed.

❋ You have to be really strict with your choice of evening bags – can you really justify buying that expensive, sparkly, tiny clutch if you can't even get your mobile phone in it?

belts

 Belts can completely change an outfit. The most versatile is a fairly wide brown leather belt with a metal buckle. This can be worn with jeans, trousers and skirts alike.

 A skinny belt looks super smart. Team a black patent skinny belt with your pencil skirt, white shirt and pointy black shoes. Gorgeous!

 Your belt should at least tone with your shoes. Never wear a black belt with brown boots or shoes. If you're going for colours or different textures, the rules are more relaxed.

sunglasses

✿ The single most important thing about sunglasses is they should protect your eyes from the sun's damaging UV rays – that's what they're for! So don't buy fashion sunglasses until you are sure they have UV protection.

✿ Big, aviator shades are really cool and they cover up a lot of your face. Perfect for those 'No photos!' moments!

✿ Classic tortoiseshell sunglasses are very Jackie O and suit everyone. Rimless, tinted shades are good all rounders.

necklaces

✽ It might sound strange but before you pick a necklace, look at your wrist! If you have little wrists, your bone structure is smaller and you will suit more delicate jewellery.

If you're slightly thicker around the wrist, you can wear cool chunky jewellery.

✽ Layering up necklaces looks really hot. Pearls look really fun when you wear strands of different lengths and colours.

✽ Boho beads give a fun look to basic jeans and T-shirt outfit. Look for wooden beads or stones like jade or amber.

earrings

❀ Earrings can be a pretty inexpensive way of really brightening up an everyday outfit or making a real glamour statement. Whatever you wear, don't go too big or wear too many pairs as they can look trashy.

❀ Vintage-style drop earrings are really hot at the moment and look fab with jeans or glam dresses, so invest in a couple of easy-to-wear pairs.

❀ If your ears aren't pierced, clip-on earrings are still an option. Get heaps of bright button earrings in fun colours. They're really inexpensive, so you can get every colour in the rainbow!

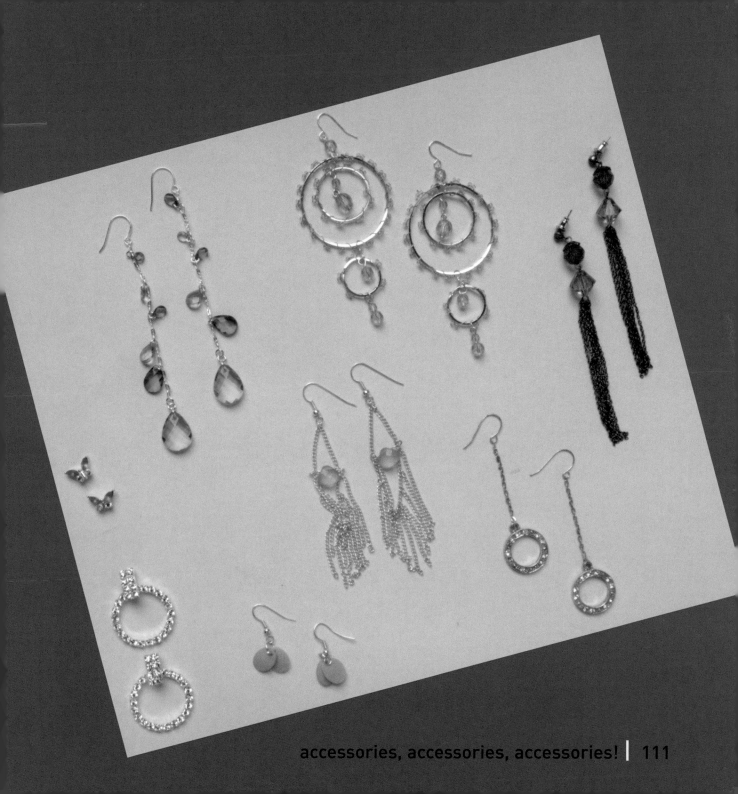

| accessories, accessories, accessories!

bracelets

✤ Bangles are really cool and like colourful earrings, they're pretty inexpensive. Rack different colours and shapes halfway up your arms or just wear one or two. It's completely up to you!

✤ Silver torque bangles and charm bracelets are a more ladylike approach to wrist wear. Both are so pretty and can be worn everyday with almost all of your outfits.

✤ For a real punk rocker look, you need leather cuffs. Try and avoid the studded look though, it's one step too far. Wear different colours and widths of leather to bring the look up to date instead.

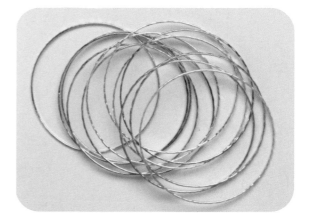

day shoes

❀ If you're going to be out and about all day, the last thing you want is skyscraper stilettos. Pointy-toed flats or kitten heels in fun colours are perfect for daywear and they come in so many styles you're bound to find the perfect pair for you.

❀ Ballet pumps are great for everyday. Comfortable and cute, they look just as good with jeans as with skirts and you can pick from dozens of cute ice cream colours.

❀ You can have as much fun with daytime shoes as with party shoes – look for fun prints like polka dots or metallic lightning bolts. Just make sure they are completely comfortable, never rely on shoes 'giving' with wear!

| accessories, accessories, accessories!

boots

✿ Simple, pointy-toed, kitten heel black leather knee boots will go with hundreds of outfits – smart with pencil skirts, rock and roll with denim skirts, neat under jeans, understated under trousers.

✿ If you can't find leather knee boots to fit, stretchy fabric boots are a great alternative and they're also a little less pricey so you can try different colours.

✿ Brown boots look best with jeans, so look for a neat pair of brown leather ankle boots to add to your collection.

hats

✳ You can have heaps of fun with hats. Even if you think hats don't suit you, maybe you're just trying the wrong shapes. Keep trying on different hats until you find one that suits you – whether it's a feathery wisp of a dress hat or a deerstalker!

✳ If you've got a small face, make sure the hat doesn't swamp you and turns up and away from your face to open it up. If you've got a larger face, you can balance it out with a larger and more dramatic hat.

✳ If in doubt, berets, beanie hats and flat caps can all look great so long as you wear them with confidence!

7 get gorgeous

"Colour plays a huge part in our wardrobes. Mary-Kate tends to experiment with bolder, brighter colors, while I usually stick to clothes in more subtle, classic shades." Ashley

This section deals with all the ways to make sure you always look your best.

If your clothes were all haute couture, you would still look drab if you weren't wearing the right colours and even a supermodel can look awkward in the wrong shapes.

Worrying whether or not you can carry off a sweeping fringe? Deliberating smokey eyes in the day? Want to buy that bright orange dress but not sure if it's your colour? Worry no more, we've got it covered.

Most fashion mistakes can be avoided by picking the right colours and shapes, so once you've read this chapter, you'll be stylish for life!

hair to suit you

* Oval face: The luckiest of all the face shapes! You can get away with most cuts and styles so make the most of it and try whatever you like!

* Round face: Try and build height into your style with layers, anything that emphasises your check bones is great. Try not to end your style at the chin as it will just make your face look rounder.

* Heart-shaped face: Your features are often quite delicate so a cute pixie crop or a bob with choppy layers will look great.

* Long face: A sweeping or even blunt fringe will look great. Avoid long, straight hair with a centre parting. Try and give your hair some shape.

all about bangs

✳ Bangs are a great way of updating your look. Don't be put off by the thought of the thick, heavy fringe that took you ages to grow out. Today's bangs are much cooler and hey, hair does grow back!

✳ Super short bangs suit oval and heart-shaped faces and they really emphasise your features.

Go for this style if you're really confident and happy to get your bangs trimmed regularly.

✳ Long sweeping bangs are the most flattering and the easiest to grow out if you change your mind. They suit most face shapes and soften your look.

casual hair

✳ Casual hair doesn't need to be pulled back into a ponytail. As long as you keep your hair in tiptop condition, there's so much you can do with your hair every day.

✳ To make a change from a ponytail, try bunches. They are really cute and keep your hair out of your face. Tie the bunches low and use invisible hair bands. NEVER elastic bands. And we are so over scrunchies.

✳ If you don't have a lot of time to style your hair, plait it into loose sections while it's damp, hit the hay and let it dry into waves overnight. When you wake up, just comb through with your fingers and smooth on some shine serum.

glam hair

✳ Sometimes it looks like people are born with glam hair but in reality it can take hours to achieve a red carpet look! Opt for something simple. You don't want to spend all evening worrying about pins falling out or gassing people with your hairspray.

✳ Straight, shiny hair always looks glamorous. Wash, deep condition and dry your hair before you hit it with the straighteners. Try and use ceramic plates, always use a protective spray or cream and use any heated appliances sparingly or you'll wreck your hair!

✳ If in doubt, pull your hair back into a low bun, sweep your fringe (if you have one) across your forehead and pull out a few tendrils to frame your face. Finish with shine serum and you're good to go.

taking care of your hair

* Try to avoid using your hair-dryer and straighteners whenever you can and let your hair dry naturally. In the long run, your hair will thank you for it!

* Stores and hairdressers are full of miracle products that promise you a thousand different things but really, all you need for the day-to-day care of your hair is shampoo, conditioner, deep conditioner and a shine serum. Anything else is just for fun!

* Once a week, try to make time for a deep conditioner to help your hair recover from heated appliance abuse! Olive oil is just as good as any store bought conditioner. Just apply to the ends of your hair and leave for ten minutes before washing off.

what colour suits me?

✳ The best way to find out which colours suit you is to tie back your hair, clean your face and hold a selection of different coloured clothes against your skin. If they suit you, they will make you look like you have peachy skin and bright eyes.

✳ Some colours will make you look like you've just got back from a great holiday, happy, relaxed and sparkling, while others will make you look grey and tired. No matter how much you love them, avoid these colours!

✳ Most people can be split into one of two categories, cool or warm. Find your ideal colour charts on the next page.

* Red is a very dynamic colour and makes you feel more energetic. As pink is a lighter shade of red, it has the same effects and makes you feel more romantic!

* Yellow is a very bright and positive colour. Wearing yellow should make you feel happy and might make you feel brainier. Yellow is said to stimulate the mind!

* Blue is very calming and perfect if you want to relax. If you've got a presentation to give, try wearing navy blue, it's perfect for confidence.

* Green is a very harmonious colour as it represents nature. It also makes quite the fashion statement!

* Orange is a very bold colour and is associated with warmth and stimulating your emotions.

* Purple is a royal colour and commands respect. It's also a very creative colour. The paler lilac is very calming and associated with the spiritual side of life, perfect for when you have some deep and meaningful thinking to do!

colour groupings
– cool

Your best colours are:
Pale blue
Mint green
Deep pink
Dark red
Purple
Silver
Turquoise

colour groupings
- warm

Your best colours are:
Deep brown
Olive green
Rust red
Gold
Burgundy
Sunshine yellow
Beige

using colour

✳ Colour make-up is fun and you can try out some new colours without buying a whole new outfit. Try a dash of bright eyeshadow or liner just on your lid to brighten up your face. Pale green, baby blue, gold and silver all look great.

✳ If you always wear a neutral or clear lip gloss, why not try some colour on your lips? Red is a great colour and despite what you might think, there is a red to suit everyone so be bold and give it a go. Just keep your cheeks and eyes neutral and if in doubt go for a transparent gloss until you feel more confident!

✳ Coloured mascaras might sound scary and insanely eighties, but they can look really hot. Blue eyes should try aubergine mascara to really bring out the blue, while a flick of blue or purple just on the tips of your lashes makes for a great flash of colour on green or brown eyed girls.

aubergine mascara

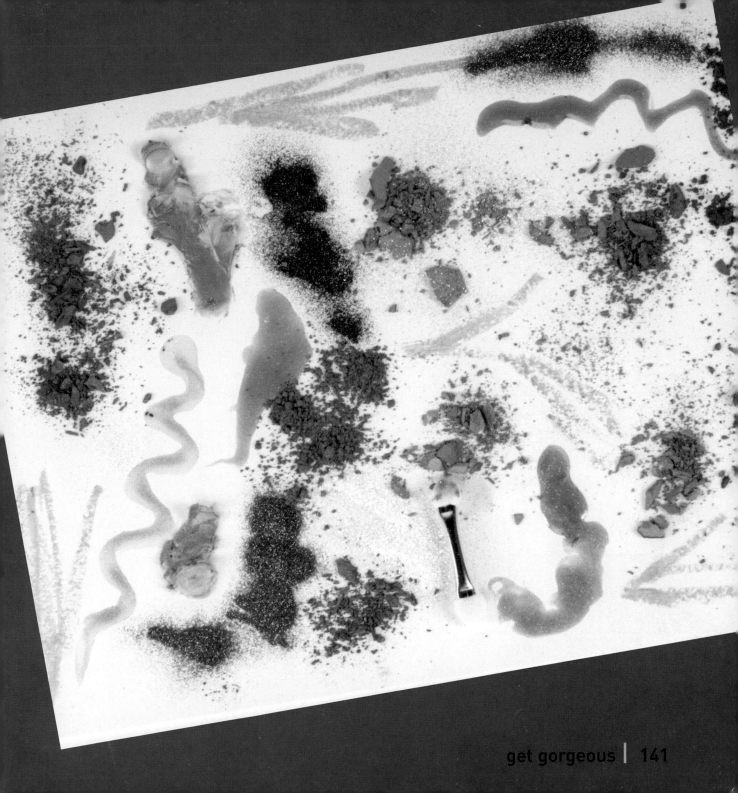

evening eyes

✳ Smokey evening eyes look great but they take a little practise. Start with a neutral base shadow, a pale grey or cream colour. Now brush on a dark grey colour in your socket line and along your lash line.

✳ Add your eyeliner, soft kohl pencil is best, along your top and bottom lash lines. The most important thing to do is blend all the hard lines away so you're left with a real smokey effect.

✳ Add a touch of pearly white highlighter just under your eyebrow and to the inner corner of your eye. Finish with a coat of black mascara and comb through with a lash comb.

neutral base:
pale grey

daytime looks

* For a cute daytime look all you really need is a clear base, defined eyelashes and a swipe of gloss. There's no point slapping on layers of make-up if you're going to be running around all day – it will only melt and you don't want to be reapplying all day.

* For a super healthy look, try a little cheek stain. It comes as a red liquid which you blend into your cheeks with your fingertips, and looks far more natural than heaps of powder on your cheeks.

* For a more natural look, try brown or clear mascara. You can even use petroleum jelly to make your lashes look glossy.

nice nails

* Looking after your nails is easy. Try not to bite them, use plenty of hand cream and never peel your polish away. Why not get in the habit of filing your nails when you're watching TV? Then it won't seem like a chore.

* Whenever you're wearing a dark colour on your nails, always wear a base coat. Black nail polish might seem rock and roll today but a stained nail bed will look terrible tomorrow.

* Give your nails a break from time to time. Gently remove any polish and use a nail buffer to smooth the nail and then buff to a natural shine.

red nail polish looks really glam!

skincare essentials

✳ Even great clothes won't save you if your skin isn't healthy. Use an all over exfoliator once a week and always moisturise when you get out of the bath or shower. Inexpensive baby oils are just as good at moisturising as expensive perfume lotions and potions.

✳ Always use a sunscreen on your face. Try and choose a daily moisturiser that contains at least an SPF 15 and always wear sunscreen all over your body if you're out in the sun.

✳ What you put in is just as important as what you put on. Try and eat five portions of fresh fruit and vegetables a day and drink lots of water to keep your skin hydrated.

No two people's style is ever the same – including ours. Ashley likes to wear simple, clean lines while Mary-Kate prefers a funky, edgy look. But, no matter what your style, don't forget the easiest secret of all: wear what you love and love what you wear! Now you know our style secrets. We hope they've inspired you, and you've enjoyed the book as much as we've enjoyed putting it together. Wear everything with confidence and have fun with fashion!

Mary-Kate Ashley

mary-kate and ashley's

Join the Club!

Collectible Membership Kit · Exclusive Photos
Downloadable Goodies & More!

visit the "Members Only" area

www.mary-kateandashley.com

www.mary-kateandashley.com brings you all
the latest news and views, sizzling style
tips and hot Hollywood happenings!

TM & © 2005 Dualstar Entertainment Group, LLC. All Rights Reserved.